THIS BOOK BELONGS TO

____

Made in the USA
Las Vegas, NV
29 April 2021

22177781R00057